HAUNTED
OUTER BANKS

HAUNTED

OUTER BANKS

GHOST STORIES, LEGENDS
& MYSTERIES

LYNDA LEE MACKEN

Haunted Outer Banks
Ghost Stories, Legends & Mysteries

Published by
Black Cat Press
Post Office Box 1466
Point Pleasant Beach, NJ 08742

ISBN 978-1-7360069-6-2

Book & Cover Design by Deb Tremper, Six Penny Graphics.
www.sixpennygraphics.com

CONTENTS

INTRODUCTION

The Outer Banks (OBX) stretch nearly 200 miles from Currituck southward to Cape Lookout. Raw, remote, windswept, and mysterious, North Carolina's expanse of barrier islands is rich with ghost stories, legends, and mysteries. "Graveyard of the Atlantic," Kill Devil Hills, The Lost Colony of Roanoke, these names alone elicit a sense of spookiness.

Much of the haunting activity on the Outer Banks is maritime-related. The barrier islands face navigational challenges posed by the Diamond Shoals area off Cape Hatteras. Off the coast, two mighty forces converge—the icy Labrador Current, surging southward, and the balmy Gulf Stream, coursing north from the tropical south. When these two currents collide, massive waves roil the ocean, especially during storms. The region is relentlessly altered by raging waters and fierce winds.

Since 1526, more than 5,000 ships have sunk in these waters causing an unknown toll in human lives. Savage storms and shifting sands contributed to the loss of life and earned the storied landscape its nickname, "Graveyard of the Atlantic."

On January 31, 1921, the schooner *Carroll A. Deering* beached on a sandbar off Cape Hatteras. The entire crew vanished, and their disappearance remains one of maritime history's most enduring mysteries.

Hurricanes are a fact of life on the Outer Banks where

frequent storms impact the islands directly. OBX lore tells of a mysterious figure known as the Gray Man of Hatteras. His shadowy form appears on Cape Hatteras beaches as an early-warning indicator prior to a hurricane.

The United States Life-Saving Service was the predecessor to today's U.S. Coast Guard. For over 40 years, brave surfmen struggled through tumultuous seas to save thousands of lives. The original Kitty Hawk lifesaving station is incorporated into today's Black Pelican restaurant. The Corolla eatery is allegedly haunted by a surfman who let his emotions get the best of him.

On December 1, 1875, the Currituck Beach Light first illuminated the northern Outer Banks between Cape Henry, Virginia, and Bodie Island Light, North Carolina. The beacon served as a ray of hope for mariners. Curiously, it's not the lighthouse that's haunted. Many say the spirit activity is centered in the enigmatic North Room of the lightkeeper's quarters.

The Currituck Beach Light is one of four paranormally charged lighthouses. Check out the specters at Bodie Island and Cape Hatteras Lighthouses. Ocracoke Lighthouse keeps the light burning for three ghosts!

A legacy of buccaneering adds to the ghostly populace. During the Golden Age of Piracy, several nefarious swashbucklers roamed OBX waters. Edward Teach, a.k.a. Blackbeard, is the most famous of them all. Blackbeard spawned a reign of terror for the coastal communities which cost him his head. Look for his headless ghost on Ocracoke.

In 1587, Roanoke Island became the site of the first European colony in North America. Among the small group of settlers was founder John White and his daughter and son-in-law, Eleanor and Ananias Dare. The couple bore a daughter, Virginia Dare, the first English child born in America. When White returned to Roanoke three years later he found the colony abandoned. All 117 men, women and children, including his daughter and granddaughter, had disappeared. On Roanoke Island, does the specter of Virginia Dare, in the guise of a white doe, still roam the tangled forests of gnarled oaks?

At the Roanoke Island Inn in Manteo, a devoted postmaster remains on duty. Neither snow nor rain nor heat nor gloom of night can prevent the diligent postal worker from carrying out his duties from beyond the grave.

These are some of the awesome spirits still lingering on the Outer Banks. There's no one answer as to why some ghosts continually wander where they met their demise. Some locations simply seem to lend themselves to hauntings, perhaps due to the dramatic or grisly events that occurred there in the past. Maybe the individuals' souls are fixed to the area emotionally, possibly they view this coastal land as a spiritual home.

The otherworldly Outer Banks possess some of the most interesting hauntings in North Carolina. Read on and travel through over 400 years of history and mystery.

☠ IMPORTANT NOTICE ☠

When visiting the Outer Banks in search of ghosts, explore only public places because trespassing on private property is *illegal* and punishable by law.

CAROVA

Wash Woods Coast Guard Station

Carova Road

Amid tangles of pine and live oak, and within earshot of the ever-rumbling surf, remain the ghosts of a once-thriving village. For nearly half a century, Wash Woods was home to a Coast Guard lifesaving station, a grocery store, two churches, a school and dozens of families. Three hundred people previously existed here. They made their living as watermen, farmers, hunting guides and lifeboatmen. History contends the settlement was established in the late 1800s by European shipwreck survivors who waded ashore and decided to stay.

In 1878, the original Coast Guard station was built south of the Virginia state line and was known as Deals Station #6. In 1883, it was renamed "Wash Woods" for the village north of the border. In 1914, the federal government laid claim to the land. Then in 1917, the U.S. Coast Guard built Wash Woods Station #166 a few miles south to replace the older station.

Prone to hurricanes and harsh weather, during the 1920s and 1930s, residents began to abandon the area due to coastal flooding. Much of the settlement washed away time and time again, hence the name "Wash Woods," making life here increasingly difficult. The Life Saving Station remained operational until 1954 or 1955.

The structure housing the Wash Woods Station served as a vacation home until 1988, when Doug and Sharon Twiddy purchased the property. The Twiddys have distinguished themselves through their commitment to historic preservation on the Outer Banks. To date, they have carefully restored nine structures including the Wash Woods Coast Guard Station which is accessible only by four-wheel-drive vehicles on Carova Beach.

The small white house and lookout tower have faced the ever-churning waters of the Atlantic ocean for over 100 years. The old dwelling once housed the brave men willing to risk their lives whenever a passing ship ran aground on the coast's treacherous shoals. Today, Wash Woods Station serves as an office for Twiddy & Company Realtors. Some say the structure is haunted.

Adventuresome vacationers have enjoyed the rustic beauty and historic character of Wash Woods. Some who stayed at the former Coast Guard Station reported strange phenomena. Lights flickered on and off by themselves. Doors slammed without explanation. Yet no one was there. No one *visible* that is, although once while sitting on the back porch, guests observed a ghostly figure floating over the deck. Some who experienced unexplainable occurrences and uncomfortable feelings at the old station changed their mind about staying there.

As more and more people witnessed inexplicable events, there seemed no other explanation other than the presence of ghosts. They named their resident spirit "Mose," (pronounced *Moh-say*), after Coast Guardsman Raymond "Mose" Williams. Mose was the son of the station's first commanding officer, and served for almost 20 years at Wash Woods. Visitors to Wash Woods have reported unusual activity including mystifying wheezing, knocking, and murmuring inside and outside of the property affirming a ghostly presence.

Mose owned a large black gelding horse and when he moved to a Knotts Island farm, he left the black horse behind. It's reported that the ghost of a black equine visits from time to time. Is he looking for his old friend?

Without doubt, the scariest stories are the ones of shipwrecks and their victims who flailed helplessly in the sea, overwhelmed by the tumultuous surf. Scores ended their lives in a watery grave.

In November 1877, the *USS Huron* became stranded 200 yards from Nags Head beach in the middle of the night. Ninety-eight people perished. Two months later, the steamship *Metropolis*, broke apart during a storm. Scores of passengers and crew drowned despite rescue efforts.

Could the ghost(s) at Wash Woods Station be otherworldly presences of shipwreck victims? Or perhaps it's the spirits of the valiant surfmen still on patrol keeping an eternal lookout for ships in distress.

COROLLA

Currituck Beach Light

1101 Corolla Village Road

In 1873, Congress appropriated funds for a lighthouse to illuminate the dark coast stretching between Cape Henry, Virginia and Bodie Island Light, North Carolina. On December 1, 1875, the Currituck Beach Light illumined the northern Outer Banks operating as a beacon of hope to mariners. Currituck is a first order light which means it utilizes the largest Fresnel lens. With a 20-second flash cycle, the light can be seen 18 nautical miles away.

Currituck was the last lighthouse built on the Outer Banks. Its brick façade remains unpainted to distinguish the light from other lighthouses in the area. The natural exterior offers visitors the chance to muse over the one million bricks required to build the 162 foot beacon which requires 220 steps up a spiral staircase to reach the lantern room.

In 1939, the light became automated. Until then, lightkeepers managed lighthouse operations. Historically, lighthouse keepers' responsibilities included trimming wicks, replenishing fuel, winding clockworks, and performing routine maintenance tasks such as cleaning lenses and windows. They were also responsible for the fog signal and the weather station, and they played a major role in search and rescue at sea.

In this case, the lighthouse itself is not haunted; it's the North Room of the light keepers quarters that possesses a haunted history.

Over the course of the years, two dozen families resided in the adjacent keepers' quarters. The keepers and their families bravely faced the challenges of living on an isolated barrier island, safeguarding the property, and ensuring the light stayed lit to aid safe navigation.

In 1916, Keeper George Garner Johnson and his family were the first to live in the light station quarters. After the death of her parents Sadie Johnson came to live with her uncle. Sadie slept in the North Room of the residence.

One day in 1927, Sadie drowned while swimming with her friends on the beach in Virginia. The Coast Guard endeavored to resuscitate her, without success. Her body was taken to Corolla for burial. Sadie's sad and premature death seemed to set in motion a series of strange and tragic circumstances surrounding the North Room.

Sometime after Sadie's passing, a friend came to stay with the family. She slept in Sadie's former bedroom. The visitor contracted a mysterious illness and died in the North Room. The last family to inhabit the house also experienced a tragedy. The lighthouse keeper's wife fell victim to tuberculosis and required confinement to her bedroom to thwart the spread of the contagious disease. Combined with her diagnosis, and without family or friends to visit her, depression set in. She too ultimately succumbed to illness in the North Room.

Someone's spirit, perhaps all of them, seems to have returned to haunt the old bedroom.

When workers labored to restore the lighthouse they experienced a certain unease when repairing the North Room. They discerned indistinguishable voices but could not determine the source of the noise. The energy in the room felt off...

In the 1980s, Lloyd Childers became the caretaker of the lighthouse and keepers' quarters. While there, Childers gave tours of the keepers' house. During these visits, some people mentioned the North Room exuded an eerie vibe. One tourist was unable to even enter the room.

These days, certain visitors to the North Room report a chilly sensation upon entering the chamber. Others feel a cold breath on their neck. A few who slept in the bedroom say their sheets were pulled. They said it felt like a child tugging at the covers to get their attention.

When the house is quiet, and seemingly unoccupied, the sound of disembodied footsteps resounds inside the dwelling. At least one person sighted a shadowy lighthouse keeper in the residence.

With so much sadness occurring here it's no wonder the energies from earlier times still permeate the atmosphere.

"The shadows, whether false or true,
I put aside a doubt which asks
'Among these phantoms what are you?'"

—Elizabeth Drew Barstow Stoddard

Whalehead Club

1100 Club Road

In the 1920s, Philadelphia industrialist Edward Collins Knight Jr. and his wife, Marie Louise, commissioned the construction of a hunting lodge on Currituck Sound. Back in the day, women were excluded from all-male clubs, so the couple built their own 21,000-square-foot manse for friends and family to hunt the teeming flocks of ducks and geese along the Atlantic Flyway.

Knight and his wife spent nine hunting seasons in the stately home. Within three weeks of arriving at their estate for their annual retreat in October 1933, the Knights abruptly left the idyllic property without explanation. They never returned. Was it ghosts who frightened them away?

During World War II, the U.S. Coast Guard leased the property and accommodated about 400 men at the site. In the late 1950s, Corolla Academy, a summer school for boys, was established on the property. The structure also remained unoccupied for several years—or did it?

Every so often, the distinct aroma of cigar smoke permeated the dining room, where a portrait of Mr. Knight, holding a cigar, hangs on the wall.

The phenomenon was first noticed in the 1960s, when the Atlantic Research Corporation used the property as a rocket fuel testing site. The company's scientists and their families were housed in the mansion. During the night, occupants awoke to the smell of smoke. Fearing a fire, they sprang into action to find the cause of the odor. Most surprisingly, they found the source hanging on the dining room wall.

In the portrait, Knight is depicted holding a cigar. Most stunningly, the lodgers watched in awe as a curious haze issued from the painting! The phenomenon happened so often, the portrait eventually needed restoration due to mysterious smoke damage. To this day, many visitors report the aroma of cigar smoke while in the dining area.

Today, the building is the centerpiece of Historic Corolla Park. Listed on the National Register of Historic Places, the sunflower-yellow mansion is a prime example of Art Nouveau architecture. The restored four-story residence includes 20 rooms, an elevator, and a 6,000 square foot basement. The 39 acres boast waterfront views, ancient live oak trees, a boathouse, and footbridge. And it's haunted.

Does Mr. Knight's spirit inhabit the Whalehead Club? No one can be entirely sure, but several souls are believed to reside here.

A young boy who toured the building became agitated after sighting a little girl in the basement who beseeched him to help her. No one other than the boy encountered the little girl that day. Some claim to hear the voice of a girl singing. Others report the elevator often descends to the basement in answer to a signal when no one exists in the cellar to call the conveyance. The haunted elevator became so troublesome the lift needed to be disabled in order to stop phantom trips between floors.

Additionally, staff members said they heard footsteps behind them as they ascended the basement stairs when they were alone. Some visitors felt a chilly breath blow across their neck.

In 2009, Coastal Paranormal Investigations researched the history of hauntings at the Whalehead Club. The ghost hunters were rewarded with the sighting of a spectral lass in the basement. Her appearance was enough to convince the paranormal investigators *not* to spend the entire night there!

> *"Whatever else, indeed, a 'ghost' may be,*
> *It is probably one of the most complex*
> *phenomena in nature."*
> —Frederick W. H. Myers

KITTY HAWK

Black Pelican Restaurant

3848 N Virginia Dare Trail N

The United States Life-Saving Service was the 19th century precursor to today's U.S. Coast Guard. For over 40 years, the brave surfmen faced turbulent seas to save thousands of lives.

Built in 1874, the original Kitty Hawk lifesaving station and later additions comprise today's (haunted) Black Pelican Restaurant.

In 1903, as the active weather bureau for the coastal area, Station Number Six played an important part in providing weather information for the Wright Brothers' flight experimentation on the sand dunes south at Kill Devil Hills. After successfully completing the first flight, Wilbur and Orville Wright, returned to the Station to telegraph the world of the birth of aviation.

Most believe the haunting activity at the Black Pelican is caused by the restless spirit of Captain Theopolis L. (T.L.) Daniels.

In 1884, the Lifesaving Station Keeper job was politically appointed, and Keeper James R. Hobbs competently held the position. Keepers typically supervised six surfmen who watched for shipwrecks atop the lookout, searched miles of sand for salvage, kept a lookout for smugglers, and rescued shipwreck victims. The area became rife with shipwrecks and earned the nickname "Graveyard of the Atlantic."

By all accounts, Hobbs was conscientious and took his responsibilities seriously. As the story goes, T.L. Daniels and Hobbs did not like each other, to put it mildly. To make matters worse, Daniels coveted the job of Station Keeper. To besmirch the keeper's reputation and fitness to perform his duties, Daniels reported Hobbs to the Lifesaving authorities for painting his personal boat with government paint. He also accused Hobbs of utilizing station personnel for labor on his farm.

To make matters worse, some say Daniels insulted Hobbs' wife by "accidentally" spitting tobacco juice on her dress.

On July 7, 1884, Lieutenant E.C. Clayton arrived at the lifesaving station to probe the allegations. It did not go well. Clayton's on-site investigation incited tensions between the short-tempered Keeper and Daniels. The two men itched for a fight. Daniels cursed at Hobbs, and the hostility escalated.

Daniels reached for his pistol and Hobbs grabbed a shotgun from the closet. As Daniels fumbled with his gun, Hobbs stepped forward and fired twice killing Daniels. The official report noted, *"He died with his revolver cocked in his hand."*

T.L. was supposedly buried at sea with no witnesses and Captain Hobbs was never tried for murder. However, in the Daniels Cemetery in Wanchese there is a gravestone to Theopolis L. Daniels from his widow, Margaret. The marker indicates he died on July 7, 1884, aged 32.

Hobbs was cleared of any wrongdoing and remained the keeper until 1891, according to records at the Outer Banks History Center.

To this day, T.L.'s spirit inhabits the Black Pelican Restaurant. A dark spot staining the old wood floor near the front desk is allegedly the spot where he fell. Certain staffers will not venture upstairs after dark in the eatery. One hostess spotted a male apparition in the dining area after closing. Could it be the spirit of T.L. Daniels, shot dead inside this building over a century ago? Some think so.

Staff and customers have seen and heard otherworldly happenings. Disembodied footsteps resound, doors mysteriously close on their own, and the lights turn on and off for no reason. Toilets flush by themselves and once a young boy exited the restroom clearly distraught at the sight of a ghost!

One of the servers spotted the spirit of an old sea captain standing at the top of the stairway. Stairways are confined spaces that trap energy, and over years of people climbing the stairs, exerting and releasing energy, there remains a storehouse of energy for spirits to use to materialize. Many people will see apparitions on stairs for this reason.

Bartenders claim ashtrays slide down the bar, bottles explode, and glasses flip over. Several say they've been shoved by unseen hands. When an icy chill fills the air, many feel afraid to be alone in the building after closing. Most blame the presence of Daniels' aggressive spirit who most suspect still covets the keeper's job.

The Legend of the Black Pelican

Pelicans represent the ability to adapt in order to survive. Spiritually, the large waterbird symbolizes the qualities of self-sacrifice, caring, and dedication. These attributes also describe the courageous men of the Kitty Hawk Lifesaving Station who continually risked their lives patrolling the Atlantic shoreline. Their vigilance was matched by a different breed—a black pelican.

In the story entitled, "The Black Pelican" by Lisa Haraburda, the author writes that the Black Pelican was first sighted during a Nor'easter, soon after the Kitty Hawk station opened. Visibility was poor, and a vessel floundered in rough seas; the ship was nearly impossible to distinguish. The Black Pelican became a guide directing the lifesaving crew to the craft in peril.

Time and again the bird easily steered the men through blinding storms and turbulent waters to struggling ships and survivors. The pelican gracefully glided over the terrified shipwreck victims as a guardian until assistance arrived. The bird's presence offered hope and encouragement that help was on the way.

On December 3, 1927, the Greek steamer, *Kyzikes*, struggled in furious seas. The 28 crewmen aboard the doomed ship recognized the Black Pelican for saving their lives as did countless other survivors.

When the Kitty Hawk Lifesaving Station closed, the Black Pelican simply vanished.

In time, the pelican population declined making the bird an endangered species. Conservation efforts proved successful, the population stabilized, and the Black Pelican again flew over Dare County waters. Mariners once more observed the black bird circle overhead during severe weather.

Coast Guard members maintain that sighting the Black Pelican in flight forewarns of possible approaching danger.

The Disappearance of Theodosia Burr

Theodosia Burr was the beloved daughter of U.S. Vice President Aaron Burr. The young woman was admired as the most educated American female of her day. In 1801, she married Joseph Alston, a wealthy landowner who became governor of South Carolina. Theodosia continued to live a life of privilege and refinement.

In 1803, Theodosia gave birth to her first child, a boy named Aaron Burr Alston. The pregnancy and birth took a toll on her already fragile health. Her physical and mental health declined even further when in June 1812, her young son died.

As an antidote, Theodosia sailed to New York to visit her father. On December 31, 1812, she sailed from Georgetown, South Carolina aboard the schooner *Patriot*. The ship left the dock and headed north but the *Patriot* and all those on board were never seen again.

Theodosia's disappearance remains a mystery. Numerous ideas exist as to what happened to the ill-fated *Patriot* and its 29-year-old upper class passenger. Logbooks from the British fleet off the coast of Cape Hatteras, noted a severe storm on January 2, 1813. The *Patriot* most likely succumbed to hurricane-force winds and sank in turbulent seas.

Theodosia

One story supporting the shipwreck theory involves a doctor named William Poole from Elizabeth City, North Carolina. While vacationing in Nags Head in 1869, he provided medical treatment to an older woman. She compensated Dr. Poole for his services with an oil painting later believed to be a portrait of Theodosia Burr Alston. According to the ailing woman, her husband found the painting aboard a beached wreckage. The picture resembles Theodosia and legend states she carried the painting on board the *Patriot* as a gift for her father.

Theodosia's memory lives on in the song "Dear Theodosia," from the Broadway musical *Hamilton*, which sparked a renewed interest in her life. Unfortunately, her mysterious fate may never come to light.

Regardless of how Theodosia met her sad and untimely end, it appears her spirit remains restless. Occasionally, on mist-laden mornings witnesses claim to see a forlorn female form in a full-length dress walking along Nags Head beaches. When approached, the ephemeral woman simply disappears into the haze. Theodosia spent three days sailing on the *Patriot*. Bathing was sporadic, people sweated, clothing went unwashed, and below deck smelled rank. All who witnessed Theodosia's pitiful phantom say they detected a distinct musky odor when her spirit was present.

The desolate denizen has been sighted many times by many people over many years.

"And now I wander all alone,
Nor heed the balmy breeze,
but list the ring dove's tender moan,
and think upon the seas."
—From *On A Friend Who Was Supposed*
To Have Suffered A Shipwreck
By Theodosia Burr Alston's friend Margaret
Blennerhasset

Bodie Island Light Station

8210 Bodie Island Lighthouse Road

Rumored to be named after the dozens of corpses that have washed ashore,[1] Bodie Island Light Station (pronounced "body") stands 156-feet tall. This is the third beacon at the location built as a guiding light. In 1847, the first structure stood a mere 54 feet. Two years later, the squat tower was abandoned when it began to lean and sink due to a weak foundation. The second lighthouse built in 1859 was destroyed during the Civil War by

---

1   Most likely, however, Bodie is the name of the individual who may have owned the land.

the Confederate Army to prevent Union soldiers from utilizing the tower as a lookout.

When the spiral staircase in the present lighthouse began to deteriorate, the stairway was cordoned off for safety reasons. A padlocked, wire cage prevented entrée to any and all interested climbers. Sightseers to the lighthouse felt mystified when visiting at this time because they clearly heard men working above them. Despite the barricade, voices and whistling emanated from the lantern room at the apex of the tower. Even National Park Service personnel could not explain the inexplicable noises occurring again and again.

Could this be the spirit of a steadfast keeper still carrying out his lighthouse duties from beyond the grave? Many paranormal investigators would call this a residual haunting.

A residual haunting is paranormal activity manifesting at the same spot over and over, playing out like a tape recording on an infinite loop. The same event unfolds when certain conditions are met, such as a specific date, or during certain weather conditions, for instance.

On the other hand, an intelligent haunting is when a spirit *wants* to be noticed and/or wishes to communicate. Such is the case at the Bodie Island Light where astoundingly the spirit of a young girl sometimes interacts with visitors. Some tourists get an eerie feeling when they sense her spirit following behind them.

Wearing an old-fashioned dress, the girl's spirit seems to know when visitors are in the area. The girl's ghostly image sometimes manifests in photos taken at the site.

HATTERAS ISLAND

The Mystery of the Schooner
Carroll A. Deering

SCHOONER ABANDONED.
Beaufort, N. C., Jan. 31.—Life
guards tonight abandoñed attempts to
reach the five-masted schooner Carrol
A. Deering, which the wind is driving
on the beach off Hatteras shoal. The
guards, despite a heavy sea, were able
during the day to get within a quarter
of a mile of the schooner and to ascer-
tain that there were no survivors
aboard. The schooner first was seen
Sunday night, stranded.

The Diamond Shoals are a constantly shifting cluster of underwater sandbars extending eight miles off Cape Hatteras. Hidden dangers are concealed beneath the waves and continuously morph in both shape and depth. Since 1526, at least 600 unwary mariners ran aground before they realized their peril on the ever-changing shoals along the cape's shoreline.

In August 1920, a five-masted schooner loaded with coal left Norfolk, Virginia, bound for Rio de Janeiro, Brazil. The ship set sail captained by William H. Merritt. Captain Merritt was a World War I hero lauded for bravery when he rescued his entire crew after a German U-boat sank his ship off Cape May, New Jersey.

During this journey, Captain Merritt fell seriously ill and disembarked in Lewes, Delaware. Captain Willis B. Wormell, a veteran seafarer, replaced Merritt on the voyage. History records Wormell's disdain for his ten-man Scandinavian crew.

On January 29, 1921, Captain Jacobson, keeper of the Cape Lookout Lightship, sighted the schooner *Carrol A. Deering* on its return voyage. A crewman hailed the lightship, and speaking through a megaphone, said the *Deering* lost its anchors. Captain Jacobson noted this, but couldn't report the incident due to a disabled radio. He later described the crew's behavior on the *Deering's* deck as suspicious. Jacobson's cryptic report amplified the ensuing mystery.

Shortly thereafter, the ship ran aground onto Diamond Shoals. When surfmen sighted the vessel in distress the rescuers desperately fought raging seas and eventually reached the troubled ship days later. They noticed the sails still set and all of the lifeboats missing. Scanning the deck for signs of life, the ship seemed abandoned.

Aboard the schooner, the rescuers were greeted by a six-toed cat and no one else; the crew was nowhere to be found. The only signs of life were food left on the galley stove, and a recently slept in bed. No personal belongings remained on board.

The fate of the *Deering's* captain and crew remains one of the most puzzling maritime mysteries in history. Five government agencies, including the FBI and Coast Guard, thoroughly investigated the disappearances yet found no answers. Some suggested stormy weather caused the crew to abandon ship and try to row the lifeboats to safety, yet the *Deering* was found on the shoals in good condition. No bodies or any other evidence ever washed ashore.

Vestiges of the wrecked schooner remained on the sand for 30 years. To further add to the *Carroll A. Deering* mystery, eerie cries and moans emanated from the remnants of the ill-fated ship.

Interestingly enough, a descendant of the polydactyl puss is sometimes spotted stalking prey near the Hatteras harbor.

The Gray Man of Hatteras

Hurricanes are a fact of North Carolina coastal life. The state is ranked fourth, after Florida, Texas, and Louisiana in the number of cyclones producing hurricane-force winds in a U.S. state. Because of its location, many hurricanes hit the Outer Banks directly. Every few years, a ferocious storm blows in from the Atlantic, slams the coast, and wreaks staggering damage.

Fueled by warm, moist air, massive tropical cyclones, a.k.a. hurricanes, form in the Gulf of Mexico, often between June and November. When these storms hit the Outer Banks, they can inflict incredible havoc for ships and sailors caught in the waves and crosswinds.

Islanders, to some extent, are fortunate because an ephemeral presence appears to forewarn the inhabitants of an approaching storm. That awe-inspiring apparition is known as the Gray Man of Hatteras.

The shadowy figure is usually spotted walking along Cape Hatteras beaches; when approached, he simply fades away. When he's seen, it's certain the impending storm will be fierce and all those who see him take his warning seriously. While some believe the Gray Man appears to warn of danger, others contend the Gray Man's appearance is a message the area will be spared the storm's impact.

During Hurricane Florence in September of 2018, the Gray Man appeared on Avalon Pier in Kill Devil Hills. His amazing apparition was caught on the pier's webcam. Forecasters predicted the Outer Banks would receive the brunt of Hurricane Florence, however, the OBX received minimal impact.

Who is this mysterious Gray Man? Some believe he's the spirit of a former resident mariner who lost his life at sea during a hurricane. They say that's the reason why he comes back to warn his fellow islanders of danger. Others say his indistinct form is an ephemeral force of nature—the storm expressing itself ahead of the powerful winds and pounding waves barreling toward the vulnerable island.

Who or whatever he is, the Gray Man of Hatteras still paces the coast in the shadow of the Cape Hatteras Lighthouse. Many changes have occurred on the island over the decades; the once lonely island is now populated with residents and thriving with tourists. Yet, the Gray Man remains remarkably constant in his otherworldly quest to warn others of danger.

BUXTON

Cape Hatteras Lighthouse

46379 Lighthouse Road

The Cape Hatteras Light is the tallest in the country and the second tallest lighthouse in the world. The first light was built on Cape Hatteras in 1803. The current beacon, however, was built in 1870. The ocean soon encroached upon the tower's base. In 1999, it was moved to more than a half mile away—a relocation of staggering proportions. Today visitors can still climb the 254 spiral steps to the top of Cape Hatteras Lighthouse.

Although located a bit further from the ocean than its previous site, the view from the top is magnificent! But for some, the Cape Hatteras Light prompts uneasy feelings. That's because it's reportedly haunted.

Sailing by the lighthouse at night, many report spotting the ghost of Theodosia Burr Alston. In 1812, Theodosia sailed from Georgetown, South Carolina aboard the schooner *Patriot*. All those on board were never seen again.

Theodosia's disappearance remains a mystery. Numerous ideas exist as to what happened to the ill-fated *Patriot* and its 29-year-old upper class passenger. The most plausible theory is the *Patriot* encountered foul weather and sank in turbulent seas. Shipwrecked near the lighthouse, her forlorn phantom is often sighted walking along the beach.

Another Cape Hatteras Lighthouse ghost story involves the legend of the ghostly cat. For more than 100 years, staff and visitors have observed a large black and white cat around the lighthouse. Nine lives indeed!

The lighthouse mascot, a 20-pound phantom puss followed the lighthouse to its new inland location. The playful feline's spirit enjoys weaving between visitor's legs and is seen inside and outside the beacon. When the cat is approached, it simply vanishes.

ROANOKE ISLAND

The Lost Colony of Roanoke

Fort Raleigh National Historic Site preserves the location of Roanoke Colony, the first English settlement in the United States. Home to the Carolina Algonquian peoples for centuries; the English landed on Roanoke Island during an exploratory voyage in 1584.

In 1587, Roanoke Island became the site of the first European colony in North America. Among the small group of settlers was founder John White and his daughter and son-in-law, Eleanor and Ananias Dare. Shortly thereafter, the couple was blessed with a daughter, Virginia Dare, the first English child born in the Western Hemisphere.

John White sailed back to England for much needed supplies and promised to return in a few months. Unfortunately, war with Spain erupted and Queen Elizabeth I needed every available sailing vessel to combat the Spanish Armada.

John White returned to Roanoke three years later and found the colony abandoned. All 117 men, women and children, including his daughter and granddaughter, had vanished. The only hint of what happened to them was the word "*Croatoan*" carved into a tree.

What precisely befell the colonists? What is the real meaning of the mysterious "*Croatoan*" message? These questions still captivate historians. Most contend the colonists went their separate ways and adapted to life with the indigenous tribes.

Years after the colony's disappearance, an enduring legend emerged about Virginia Dare.

The White Doe of Roanoke

Virginia Dare spent her childhood in the tribe of the friendly Indian Manteo. Now known as Winona-Ska, the first born English child in North America, grew into a beautiful young woman.

Okisko was a handsome young chieftain who wanted Winona-Ska as his wife. However, an old witch doctor, Chico, also wished to marry Winona-Ska. Chico became jealous of Okisko. When Winona-Ska rebuffed Chico's romantic interest, the infuriated witch doctor used his magic and turned her into a white doe. If he couldn't have her, no man would.

Okisko became focused on reversing the curse placed by Chico. Tribal magician, Wenokan, helped him craft a special arrow with an oyster shell tip. He and Wenokan took the arrow to a magic fountain, dipped the arrow into the water, and the arrow tip became pearl. If the white doe was shot with the pearl arrow, the evil spell would be broken, and Winona-Ska would become human again.

At the same time, Wanchese decided to seek admiration by killing the enchanted white doe. He knew only a silver arrow could kill this special animal. His father, also named Wanchese, was the Indian who traveled to England with Manteo. Queen Elizabeth I gave a silver arrow to Wanchese and now the son would use the weapon to kill the white doe.

One day Okisko spotted the white doe near the ruins of the English settlement on Roanoke Island. He aimed his magic pearl arrow… Simultaneously, Wanchese shot his silver arrow from another direction. Both arrows pierced the white doe's heart. Okisko's pearl arrow transformed Winona-Ska back into a beautiful young woman, but Wanchese's silver arrow pierced her human heart. Okisko rushed to her, but Winona-Ska died in his arms.

Hunters routinely reported seeing a white doe until the 20th century. Some said they discerned the white doe whisper, "*Virginia Dare.*"

In the essay "The Disappearance of Roanoke Colony: What Happened to Virginia Dare?" the author states that other legends concerning rare, white animals describe these elusive creatures as "shapeshifting witches,"[2] transforming their physical form at will.

2   Otherworldly Oracle, www.otherworldlyoracle,com, June 13, 2019.

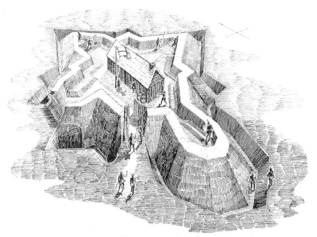

FIGURE 1—Artist's reconstruction of the fort

Fort Raleigh National Historic Site protects, and preserves known portions of England's first New World settlements from 1584 to 1590. The site also conserves the cultural heritage of the Native Americans, European Americans and African Americans who have lived on Roanoke Island. For additional information contact:

Fort Raleigh National Historic Site
1401 National Park Drive
Manteo , NC 27954
Phone: 252-472-2111

MANTEO

Roanoke Island Inn

305 Fernando Street

In the 1860s, Asa and Martha Jones built a simple island house on what is now Fernando Street. Asa salvaged wood from shipwrecks to construct the dwelling. Over a century later, the Roanoke Island Inn more than doubled in size from its original structure.

In the early 1900s, in addition to lodging guests, the property also housed the post office. The Roanoke Island Inn, as it stands today on the Manteo Waterfront, opened in 1990, and is remarkably associated with tales of strange phenomena around the property.

As the story goes, Jones' son Roscoe was a well-respected postal worker. The Outer Banks History Center website features Roscoe's "Postmaster Appointment Certificate." Roscoe served as the first Postmaster of Griffin on Nags Head's sound-side, and later as Manteo Postmaster from 1922 until 1934.

Shortly after Roscoe's passing, reports of a male apparition wearing a postal worker's uniform, was seen leaving and entering the inn's front door. Some observed the curious spirit walking toward the post office. All who witnessed the vision claimed the specter bore a striking resemblance to Roscoe Jones.

Innkeepers and guests reported the sound of disembodied footsteps walking back and forth upstairs. Other unexplainable anomalies included radios turning on and off, blinds moving by themselves, and vases mysteriously falling and shattering on the floor. Is Roscoe's ghost to blame for these other oddities?

"Neither snow nor rain nor heat nor gloom of night stays these couriers from the swift completion of their appointed rounds," is the postal worker's creed. Some would say Roscoe's spirit took the slogan literally and to a much loftier level.

The Pioneer Theatre

113 Budleigh Street

A common superstition is that every theater possesses a ghost. We attend the theater for all kinds of thrills—romance, suspense, and unexpected plot twists. But theaters themselves, with their long histories of players, staff, and patrons coming and going, are the stuff of legend. It could be because the buildings tend to be old and creaky. Either way, the Outer Banks boasted a haunted theater...

In 1918, the Pioneer Theatre opened and presented silent films. Two local women provided piano music accompaniment. The theater on Sir Walter Raleigh Street soon became a cultural and social center. In 1934, the playhouse moved to Budleigh Street.

In 1957, Andy Griffith, who lived on Roanoke Island, attended the opening of his debut film, *A Face in the Crowd*, at the theater. Griffith is a hometown hero and became well-known for his TV program, "The Andy Griffith Show," which aired from 1960 to 1968.

This landmark movie house was said to be haunted by the spirits of former family members who seemingly continued working at the theater. They passed on but did not leave the confines of the cozy cinema. Some moviegoers said when they attempted to use their cell phone, a cool, phantom hand on their shoulder was a gentle postmortem reminder to put the phone down and focus on the movie screen.

Over the years, unusual numbers of orbs appeared in photos taken inside the venue. Paranormal investigators contend orbs are a form of energy that a spirit or other entity can use to manifest. Some of the light spheres contained faces within the globule.

Sadly, as of this writing, the landmark, and spirit filled, theater closed its doors after more than 100 years.

> *"We leave quite soon, the way we came,*
> *the theatre ghosts are gone.*
> *Their secrets hidden from our eyes,*
> *their haunting days are done."*
> —Dindleh, from "Most Haunted Theatre"

The Tranquil House Inn

405 Queen Elizabeth Avenue

The Tranquil House Inn is nicely situated on Manteo's historic waterfront on Roanoke Island. The celebrated inn is conveniently located and features unobstructed views of Shallowbag Bay.

The guesthouse also offers a bit of the extraordinary...

Some of the lodgers claim to hear disembodied footsteps and slamming doors, Lights turn on at will, as if flicked on by a ghostly hand. Another eerie disturbance is televisions turn on and off in every room without the benefit of human hands. Even though new televisions were purchased, the eerie phenomenon continued.

A spirit meddling with technology is common. Spirit is an energy current and quite capable of disrupting other energy currents. Why do they do it? Sometimes Spirit interferes with electricity to get our attention, to let us know they're here. Or they might be trying to deliver a message.

The first floor seems to elicit the most haunting activity. Astoundingly, the visage of a female apparition sometimes materializes in mirrors. Once a female guest observed a ghostly woman next to her bed. According to *Ghosts of the Outer Banks* by Peggy Schmidt, the woman who sighted the spirit recognized the interloper as an otherworldly figure because of the outdated clothing she wore. Every time the guest attempted to get out of bed, the female phantom pushed her back down! When the guest commanded the ghost to "*Stop!,*" the apparition vanished.

There are some who say a perturbed spirit insists the toilet seat be kept down and slams the lid to emphatically make her point.

"Here groves embowered and more sequestered shades,
Frequented by the ghosts of ancient maids,
Are seen to rise. The melancholy scene,
With gloomy haunts and twilight walks between."
—Thomas Gray

OCRACOKE ISLAND

Blackbeard's Ghost

During the Golden Age of Piracy, several nefarious pirates roamed the waters off the Outer Banks. Captain Kidd, Calico Jack, Black Bellamy and the most notorious Blackbeard, a.k.a. Edward Teach, spawned a reign of terror for the coastal communities.

Blackbeard stood six-foot, five-inches tall and towered over his opponents. Dressed in all black, he tied colored ribbons in his long black beard. He'd ignite slow burning cannon fuses and hide them in his whiskers. With a billow of smoke encircling his head, most times his terrifying presence triggered his victims to surrender without a fight.

Occasionally, he set fire to his rum using gunpowder, and drank it, flames and all.

By 1718, Blackbeard regarded Ocracoke as his favorite anchorage and often lodged at the landmark "White House," today's Hammock House. When he hosted a days-long party for his rowdy buccaneer associates, residents complained to Virginia Governor Alexander Spotswood. The governor immediately dispatched two sloops, commanded by Lieutenant Robert Maynard of the Royal Navy, to sail to Ocracoke and put an end to Blackbeard's intimidations once and for all.

In the deep water channel off Springer's Point, a battle ensued between Blackbeard and his crew, and Maynard and his men. The bloody, hand-to-hand conflict resulted in Maynard vanquishing Blackbeard's crew. Blackbeard suffered 25 wounds from pistols, swords, and daggers yet he fought on as blood spurted from his body. On November 22, 1718, the infamous buccaneer's reign of terror dramatically ended upon his beheading.

Legends says after Maynard tossed Blackbeard's corpse into the water, the crew watched in awe as Blackbeard's headless body swam around the ship three times before finally succumbing to the depths. Lieutenant Maynard sailed out of Teach's Hole dangling Blackbeard's head from the sloop's bow symbolizing the death of piracy.

Some say Blackbeard's body eventually washed ashore and was buried in a secret location. His storied skull vanished in London around 1840. Carolinian lore contends pirates stole Blackbeard's skull and fashioned the head into a drinking bowl. Some say the vessel was coated in silver and engraved with the words "*Deth to Spotswoode.*"

Although Blackbeard's death ended an era, his legend lives on. In the early 1800s, locals began to sight spectral ships and hear phantom sounds of conflict. Witnesses observed enormous balls of fire streaming back and forth across the water.

Ocracokers and residents of neighboring islands claimed anytime a storm approached, Blackbeard's full-bodied apparition manifested on the beach. Some believe Blackbeard's ghost appears during storms because he remains on the hunt for his missing head; he hopes the roiling waters will churn up his skull.

Often, his ghost appears with a strange light where his head would be; this phenomenon is referred to as "Teach's Light." Those in the know claim Blackbeard's ghost commonly roams the shore along Teach's Hole. The phantom pirate holds a lantern aloft and appears to be looking for his severed head.

Ocracoke Lighthouse

Lighthouse Road

O cracoke Lighthouse is the oldest operating lighthouse in North Carolina. In 1822, Congress set aside $20,000 for a lighthouse on the island. Noah Porter of Massachusetts completed the tower and keeper's cottage well underbudget for a total of $11,359. That's startling in itself, but there's more. The original whitewash "recipe" called for blending lime, salt, whiting, rice, glue, and boiling water. The mixture was applied to the bricks while still hot.

The lighthouse survived the Civil War with minimal damage; Confederate troops dismantled the fourth order Fresnel lens in 1862, but Union forces re-installed the lens the following year. The light was electrified in the early 1900s and today casts a steady beam visible for fourteen miles.

Also visible is an unknown phantom who appears dressed in a light blue gown. Her awesome apparition usually appears after evening thunderstorms. Occasionally, she even says *"hello"* to passersby. The female ghost is described as pretty, with long dark hair and olive skin, and she sometimes materializes carrying a lantern.

Theodosia Burr Alston lost her life when the *Patriot*, the ship she sailed on, vanished off the Outer Banks. Her spirit emerges near the lighthouse as well. She wears a full-length, white frock and witnesses say her specter displays dripping wet hair laced with seaweed. Her appearance is accompanied by a strong, musty smell.

Last but not least, is the wraith of a bearded, lighthouse keeper wearing black and gray striped trousers and a white shirt. His long hair is often tied with a black string. The keeper's apparition appears as solid as a living, breathing person until he walks through people and other dense impediments in his path.

"We shall not know the ships that lie
Deep sunk upon their shifting floors
Nor whose the ghost that flit and fly
Upon their thousand-sided shores."

—J.F. Dahlgren

David Williams House

49 Water Plant Road

Since 1992, the Ocracoke Preservation Society has called the historic David Williams House their home. The structure and surrounding Ocracoke Historic District property are on the National Register of Historic Places.

This traditional two-story house was built around 1900. Its owner, David Williams, served as the first Captain of the U.S. Coast Guard unit in Ocracoke Village when the Coast Guard replaced the U.S. Lifesaving Service in 1915.

In 1989, the house was moved to its present location on National Park Service property. The Ocracoke Preservation Society preserved and restored the historic dwelling.

The ground floor rooms serve as a museum and display historical exhibits bringing the past to life, so to speak. And it seems to be working... The second floor accommodates a research library and administrative offices. The top story also houses a ghost. The phantom manifests as an elderly man dressed in vintage clothing.

In *Lighthouse Ghosts & Carolina Coastal Legends*, authors Norma Elizabeth and Bruce Roberts share a description of the mysterious man who appears in the upper right hand window. They reveal the apparition is an old man with a big, bushy beard. He wears an old-fashioned coat and a stovepipe hat and enfolds a terrier dog in his left arm.

Visitors are always encouraged to look at the window to see if they can spot the apparition who mostly emerges on atmospheric, overcast days. Many have been rewarded with a sighting so why not take a look for yourself!

Island Inn

25 Lighthouse Road

Ocracoke is the most southern island on the Cape Hatteras National Seashore. Accessible only by ferry, boat, or plane, embarking upon the 9.6 mile island, visitors enter an historic, isolated, and otherworldly isle…

In 1901, the Ocracoke Lodge of the Independent Order of Odd Fellows[3] purchased one acre of land where they built a two-story structure constructed entirely from wood salvaged from shipwrecks. The first floor accommodated the village schoolhouse and the upper floor functioned as the Odd Fellows meeting space.

After about 25 years, the lodge disbanded and in 1940, Stanley Wahab bought the building. He opened Wahab Coffee Shop which encompassed a soda fountain and an ice cream parlor. During World War II, the Coast Guard Station became the post for the U.S. Navy. Naval Officers were quartered on the building's second floor fittingly called the "Crow's Nest."

Wahab eventually added extensions and the building became the island's first modern hotel, the Silver Lake Inn. The hotel featured indoor plumbing, electricity, a contemporary kitchen and dining room. On Saturday nights, the hostelry became a popular gathering spot hosting square dances and other island events.

During the war, Mr. and Mrs. Godfrey managed the inn for Wahab. The couple "fought like cats and dogs" everyone said, so when Mrs. Godfrey failed to return from the mainland, eyebrows raised. Horror struck all who knew her when her mutilated body was found on Cedar Island. No one was ever charged with her murder.

Did this injustice cause her spirit to stay behind and torment her husband? Throughout the day Mr. Godfrey spotted her specter walking about the inn. At night he observed her ghostly presence

3   The historic command of the Order of Odd Fellows is to *"visit the sick, relieve the distressed, bury the dead, and educate the orphan."* The organization focuses on helping the community and making the world a better place.

in his room glaring at him. Doors began to open, and slam shut for no reason. Disembodied footsteps resounded on the staircase. Mrs. Godfrey's ghostly presence became too much for her husband to bear so he quit his job and moved back to the mainland.

Room 21 (some say Room 23) seemed to be the epicenter of the haunting activity. Objects moved and/or went missing only to reappear in other parts of the inn. Faucets turned on and off on their own. Toilet paper rolls unfurled, and doors opened and closed without benefit of human hand. Pictures hanging on the wall went askew and inexplicable sounds occurred, their source unknown.

The most spectacular manifestation was the materialization of Mrs. Godfrey's full-bodied apparition. When she appeared it looked as if she was tucking visitors in their bed! Some of her other post-mortem antics included sitting on lodgers' beds. Her presence was literally felt when the wraith reached out her phantom hand and grabbed a sleeping guest's toe.

When the Great Lakes Paranormal Society explored the Island Inn in October 2020, they recorded Mrs. Godfrey's voice. After an investigator pronounced, *"It's a beautiful hotel,"* a female voice responded, *"Tell people that I am alive."*

It's totally understandable that some felt a sense of unease, to put it mildly, after encountering Mrs. Godfrey's ghost. Many asked for a change of room. The innkeepers always happily accommodated their guests.

In 2018, the Ocracoke Preservation Society purchased the inn building. Plans are underway to restore the original 1901 structure which housed the Odd Fellows Lodge and School; the two wing sections were demolished. The building is slated to serve as a community visitors center. It will be interesting to see if Mrs. Godfrey's ghost approves of the changes.

"If we could take a material man and dissolve away his physical constituent without interfering with the sense-data by means of which we perceive him, we should be left with, exactly, an apparition."
—G.N.M. Tyrell, *Apparitions*

Old Diver

Augustus Abner McGuire (1856–1913) was an Irish American seafarer and diver who worked on schooners and other sailing vessels along the East Coast.

In 1913, McGuire served as a suit diver aboard a Norwegian ship which sprang a leak while sailing past Ocracoke Island. McGuire was outfitted in a brass diving helmet, and waterproof suit, with a long air tube attached enabling his immersion underwater. When he submerged to repair the breach, something went horribly wrong. Somehow McGuire's diving apparatus malfunctioned, and he was left without oxygen; others say McGuire suffered a heart attack. When crew members pulled McGuire to the surface the diver was unresponsive. The captain and crew did all they could to resuscitate him, but to no avail.

Instead of conducting a burial at sea, the captain contacted the Ocracoke Lifesaving Station. Keeper David Williams acquired a burial plot outside his family graveyard. The Methodist preacher performed a simple and dignified funeral service for the diver. Kind-hearted islanders gathered and paid respect to a man they never knew.

A cedar post served as McGuire's headstone and his weighted diving boots were placed at the foot of the grave. Eventually the cedar post rotted away, and the weighted boots were removed. You can see the Old Diver's boots on display at the Ocracoke Preservation Society's Museum.

Shortly after the diver's burial, islanders began to sense the Old Diver's ghost haunted the sandy lane near his grave. Sometimes at twilight, his specter ambled along the gritty path, plodding along in his diving suit and helmet, his weighted feet slowly making his way down the road. Was his restless spirit seeking to return to his native Ireland?

For many years, people thought twice before walking by the boneyard after dark. Most say the Old Diver's ghost may still appear to those who believe in him. Check out his grave at night, if you dare…

Another old diver—the author's father, Edmund Charles Macken, U.S. Navy Diver, 1944.

MOREHEAD CITY

The Old Webb Memorial Library

812 Evans Street

In 1929, Morehead City native Earle W. Webb, Sr., was the chief executive of Ethyl Corporation in New York City. He commissioned a commercial building in downtown Morehead

City. The edifice replaced the Wade House that originally stood on the site.[4] The first floor served as doctors' offices while the upper floor housed a training facility for local garment workers.

Eventually, the upstairs noise became too distracting for the doctors, so the business relocated. Mrs. Webb offered the second floor space to the Morehead Women's Club to use for its 300 volume lending library.

4   The storied Wade House was already the subject of ill-founded gossip and legend.

In 1936, tragedy struck the family when Earle Jr. became ill with lung disease and died; he was only 19 years of age. To honor their son, the Webbs donated the building to Morehead City for use as the Earle W. Webb Jr. Memorial Library and Civic Center.

The first night paranormal investigators Joey and Tonya Madia visited the Webb Library they encountered several spirits. The couple's investigation eventually lasted for over two years and included 70 nights and 150 hours of research. They amassed so much evidence they ultimately authored a book about their findings at the library entitled, *Watch Out for the Hallway: Our Two-Year Investigation of the Most Haunted Library in North Carolina.* They claimed the Webb was the most paranormally active site they ever encountered which begs the question:

Why is the old Webb Memorial Library building so haunted?

Feng shui is an ancient Chinese practice which uses energy forces to harmonize individuals with their environment. Feng shui literally means "wind-water." Since ancient times, landscapes and bodies of water were thought to direct the flow of universal energy through places and structures.

The Madias say that according to Feng shui, the two windows facing each other in the upstairs hallway serve to thin the veil between dimensions. The window placement created a gateway or a portal enabling the spirits to pass through more easily. Tonya is a psychic medium; her sensitive energy attracts the paranormal. She called the passageway the "Grand Central Station" of ghosts and discerned rows upon rows of spirits walking the upstairs corridor.

A Spirit Box a.k.a. a Ghost Box, is a machine that enables verbal communications from spirits. Utilizing the device, a variety of entities, male, female, young, and old souls, communicated with the paranormal investigators and validated that the second floor hallway is indeed a gateway for the spirits.

Some ghost hunters contend that water acts as a conduit for paranormal phenomena. A water source near a haunted location could potentially be fueling the eerie activity. Morehead City marks the confluence of the Newport River, Bogue Sound and Beaufort Inlet.

Joey and Tonya found that much of the haunting activity at the Webb is maritime related. The region is known as the "Graveyard of the Atlantic" due to savage storms and shifting sandbars that caused 5,000 shipwrecks and tremendous loss of life. The area possesses a legacy of piracy adding to the ghostly populace.

Another factor for the phantom activity is a hospital once operated nearby; the building currently serves as a nursing home. Incredibly, investigators even encountered spirits from the neighboring edifice. Also, two doctor's offices once existed in the Webb building. A place that is haunted can be associated with strong emotions; sickness, death, and grief transpired in both structures adding to the number of spirits.

According to mediums, one of the more nefarious spirits haunting the building is a textile merchant who ran the training facility upstairs. Female clairvoyants encountered his spirit many times and discerned a phantom hand on their legs. They even felt their bottoms pinched!

Oddly enough, the Madias never encountered any member of the Webb family.

When the building underwent remodeling, the supernatural activity turned up a notch. Spirits, like the physical beings they once were, dislike changes in their environment and oftentimes will show their perturbance. When an elevator was installed in the building to comply with the Americans with Disabilities Act, light orbs became evident with the naked eye as well as being captured on camera. The lift seemed to host a different level of strangeness. Maybe the existence of the new-fangled convenience in their midst offered a unique interest for the spirits.

The Town of Morehead City moved library operations to 202 S 8th Street in January 2022. This writer suspects the phantom population stayed behind at their perfectly proportioned portal.

BEAUFORT

Hammock House

1117 Hammock Lane

Private Residence*

stablished in 1713, Beaufort is the fourth oldest town in North Carolina. However, it's history dates to the late 1600s when Native Americans subsisted here. Originally known as Fishtown, the place was eventually renamed for the Duke of Beaufort, Henry Somerset.

The 1709 Hammock House is Beaufort's oldest building. The structure originally served as an inn and appeared on area maps as "The White House." The dwelling was eventually renamed the "Hammock House" because of its location on a hill or "hummock." In earlier days, the two-storied landmark served as a navigational aid for ships arriving into port.

There are many legends and stories connected with the house. Some people claim the house is haunted because, at times, the sound of festive parties, laughs, screams, and the clashing of swords can be heard. These residual hauntings may be attributed to "place memory" a concept put forth by the Society for Paranormal Research in 1885.

Place memory is a theory that suggests traces of memory might affix themselves to certain objects. The Hammock House retains some of its original woodwork, such as beams and floors. The energy of events that transpired in the structure may be imbedded and sensitive individuals may be able to decipher, feel, hear, or perceive past occurrences.

"The air itself is one vast library, on whose pages are for ever written all that man has ever said or women whispered. There, in their mutable but unerring characters, mixed with the earliest, as well as with the latest sighs of mortality, stand forever recorded, vows unredeemed, promises unfulfilled, perpetuating in the united movements of each particle, the testimony of man's changeful will."
—Mathematician Charles Babbage, 1838

Blackbeard lodged at the inn during his stopovers in Beaufort. Legend says he enjoyed the company of an 18-year-old French woman while there. Some say she was his common-law wife and, allegedly, not a willing one. Blackbeard became so irate with her disinterest that when he set off for the sea he ordered her to hang on an oak tree in the front yard. When the moon is full, people say her screams can still be heard.

Another oft told tale involves Richard Russell, Jr., who, upon his return from sea, forced a slave to the Hammock House attic to punish him. The slave overpowered Russell and pushed him down the stairs. Russell broke his neck and according to some, his spirit remains.

During the Civil War Union officers were billeted in the house. When three of the officers left their quarters, they were never seen again. That is until 1915, when workmen digging near the back porch found remains of three men; their intact buttons and buckles identified them as Civil War era soldiers.

So many tragic stories were associated with the house that many citizens became apprehensive. Was the old place haunted? For years, the Hammock House sat vacant. Or did it? The vandalism and neglect inflicted on the deteriorating structure over the years added fuel to haunting stories.

Another discomfiting tale involves Captain Madison Brothers who became engaged to Samantha Ashby, the orphaned daughter of a wealthy Baltimore family. Upon his arrival in Beaufort, the

Captain noticed a jovial party in the Hammock House Inn and witnessed his betrothed dancing with another man. The Captain possessed a fierce temper earning him the nickname "Mad" Brothers. Upon seeing Samantha in the arms of a handsome sailor he flew into a blind rage.

Unbeknownst to the Captain the young man his fiancée danced with was Lieutenant Carruthers Ashby, Samantha's brother. Swords clashed as the two men doggedly battled each other. The guests watched in horror and were warned off—the Captain deaf to their cries that he was making a mistake.

The Captain forcefully pursued Ashby across the ballroom and up the stairs. Ashby was cornered and his only choice was to lunge at his opponent. He lost his balance and fell on his back. The seething Captain drew a knife from his belt and stabbed Ashby through the heart.

Some say to this day, traces of the victim's blood remain on the treads of the steps.

With his dying breath, Lieutenant Ashby requested to be buried in full dress uniform, standing at attention, in the direction of his British homeland.

Lieutenant Ashby's grave is among the more unusual graves in Beaufort's Old Burying Ground. The naval officer is buried in an upright coffin, facing home to England. However, the grave marker doesn't give the name of the grave's occupant, only stating, *British Naval Officer, buried standing in salute to His Majesty King George 3rd.*

*Private residence.
Trespassing is illegal and strictly forbidden. ☠

Old Burying Ground Cemetery

400 Ann Street

*"Graveyards exist as the place where the
living contemplate the mysteries, traumas
and heartbreaks associated with death."*
— Robert Lamb

The Old Burying Ground Cemetery is located near the Hammock
House on Ann Street in Beaufort's historic district. The town's
oldest cemetery holds layer upon layer of Beaufort's 300 year history.

Many who visit the Old Burying Ground feel a sense of
fear and unease. Others say the burial ground is one of the eeriest

and most unsettling cemeteries they have ever visited and swear it's haunted. Visitors often feel compelled to look over their shoulder as they sense someone, or something, following close on their heels.

Established in the early 1700's, the cemetery's weathered tombstones chronicle the coastal town's heritage. Captain Otway Burns (1775–1850) one of North Carolina's greatest naval heroes in the War of 1812, is interred here. A cannon taken from his privateer, *Snapdragon*, is mounted on his marble tomb.

North Carolina's coast is aptly named the "Graveyard of the Atlantic," since thousands of ships and lives have been lost at sea during the past three centuries. The victims of the *Crissie Wright* shipwreck are buried in a common grave here. Only one seafarer survived the disaster; six crew members drowned or froze to death after their schooner went aground at Shackleford Banks in January 1886. "Cold as the night the *Crissie Wright* came ashore" was a phrase Beaufort natives used to describe extreme, frigid weather. Mercifully, this tragedy led to the establishment of the Cape Lookout Lifesaving Station in 1887.

In the 1700s, an English family, including an infant daughter, came to reside in Beaufort. When the girl grew older she expressed a desire to visit her homeland. Her mother reluctantly agreed to the trip. Her father promised his wife that he and the girl would return safely. The daughter enjoyed her visit to London, but she fell ill on the voyage home and passed away. Normally, she would have been buried at sea, but her father insisted he keep his promise to bring her home. He purchased a barrel of rum from the captain and placed her body in the cask to preserve her remains for burial at Beaufort.

Visitors often leave gifts of shells, toys, and other objects atop her grave, which is marked by a piece of wood. Several people claimed to have spotted a spectral girl playing in the cemetery at night. Some say the girl's spirit sometimes leaves one of her gifted tokens in other sections of the cemetery.

The little girl in the rum cask is not the only spirit haunting this graveyard, which was deeded to the town in 1731. The cemetery is also the final resting place of Revolutionary and Civil War soldiers, settlers killed during the Tuscarora War (1711–1715), and other restless souls of Beaufort's past.

ATLANTIC BEACH

Fort Macon State Park

2303 East Fort Macon Road

The now peaceful and picturesque Fort Macon State Park began its existence as a contrivance of war. The War of 1812 provoked the United States to build a line of defenses along the Eastern Seaboard to secure the coastline. In 1826, the U.S. Army Corp of Engineers began construction on Fort Macon.

Fort Macon's purpose was to guard Beaufort Inlet and Beaufort Harbor, North Carolina's only major deepwater ocean port. The five-sided fort took eight years to construct and was named for the eminent North Carolina statesman Nathaniel Macon. Built of brick and stone, the citadel contains 2,379,546 bricks—more than any other U.S. fort. Twenty-six vaulted rooms, called casements, comprise the substantial stronghold constructed with five-foot thick walls.

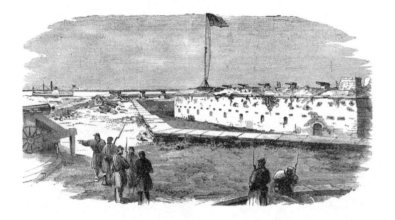

At the onset of the Civil War, the North Carolina Confederacy wrestled the port from Union soldiers. In 1862, the tables turned, and Union forces attacked the fort, but the Confederate soldiers refused to capitulate. Besieged by relentless gunfire for 11 hours straight, cannon fire struck the fortress more than 560 times. By the next day, the commander, Colonel Moses J. White held no choice but to raise the white flag in surrender.

The fortification went on to serve as a federal prison for both civil and military personnel from 1867 to 1876. Fort Macon officially closed in 1903.

Twenty years later, the State of North Carolina purchased the fort from the federal government and transformed the location into a state park. The citadel became reactivated as a coastal defense for a short while during World War II.

Fort Macon is faithfully restored and one of the most visited parks in the state, reportedly receiving more than one million visitors each year, undoubtedly due to its beautiful setting.

Some visitors to the park allege Civil War spirits haunt the citadel. Those who've sighted the spectral soldiers identify the souls as Confederates. Are these otherworldly compatriots keeping a lookout for approaching Union fighters?

During the Siege of Fort Macon in 1862, Confederate soldier Benjamin Combs met an untimely death. The young soldier's back was struck by a mortar shell. Combs suffered for five agonizing days before succumbing to death. Is it Benjamin Combs' ghost patrolling the fortification and watching for attackers?

Combs' spirit is accused of sometimes slamming doors, locking rooms, and switching off the lights—much to everyone's surprise. When he's commanded to *"Cut it out!"* he readily obeys.

Perhaps the spirits are former prisoners. Witnesses report seeing troops marshaled outside the fort. Is it their spirits who move objects within the fort only to have them reappear somewhere else inside the stockade? Disembodied footsteps resound, phantom gunfire resonates, and the sound of men speaking, although incoherently, echoes.

There exists a parapsychological theory called "place memory" which states an environment can store the essence of human activity and communications. Most times, the events recorded are intensely emotional, including untimely death. What can be more extreme than an 11-day bombardment or incarceration in a 19th century prison?

Embedded energy can remain for years, even centuries, which corresponds to the reports of apparitions, audible communications, and other paranormal events at Fort Macon. According to place memory, the environment can be viewed, heard, tasted, smelled, or felt at a later time period by sensitive individuals.

A Psychic Medium Gets Punched in the Gut

"When my son married a girl from Atlantic Beach, I acquainted myself with the nearby area. After the wedding, we took several guests and family members on a tour which included Fort Macon State Park. I found the fort interesting and so well preserved. We were all impressed at how well kept both the grounds and buildings were.

As an empath, I am always curious to see if there are any obvious indications of energy lingering at historic sites. Fort Macon did not disappoint.

It was a beautiful, sunny September day, as we walked around the fort enjoying the grounds, and observing all the different rooms called casements. I felt a few tingles of unusual energy but not anything major until we were about to enter another room. As I stepped into the space, I literally felt punched in the stomach. I was knocked backward and let out a loud, "oomph," in reaction. I ran out of the room and the three people with me became so concerned they stayed with me as I tried to recover and catch my breath.

When I got my breath back, I tried to discern who or what struck me. I remembered a plaque on the wall that said the room was where prisoners were held. I found out later that because there were no state or federal *penitentiaries, Fort Macon was used for about 11 years as a civil and federal prison.*

I experienced similar physical reactions at other historic places. As I walked the woods in Leesburg, Virginia, at one point I suddenly could go no further. I needed to turn around because I felt so sick to my stomach. Such sad energy abounded. When visiting London, England, I was stopped in my tracks as I approached the infamous Tower of London. I waited outside to try to regain my mental and physical equilibrium."

—Bobbi Torres

"Thin, airy shoals of visionary ghosts."
—Homer, *The Odyssey*

ACKNOWLEDGEMENTS

Many thanks to Hendrix, Mackey, Jalayne, and Beau Torres. My Morehead City family went out of their way to capture evocative photos at Fort Macon and the old Webb Library. I greatly appreciate your efforts.

I am grateful to Bobbi Torres for being the best sounding board and for sharing her haunting experiences.

Oceans of gratitude to Graphic Designer Debra Tremper. Deb has designed my ghost books for over twenty years. Once again, this talented collaborator created another dynamic cover and interior layout.

I value the dedication of all the paranormal investigators, photographers, psychic mediums, researchers, and writers who pursue the paranormal. You inspire so many, including me.

Finally and importantly, my appreciation for all of my readers is as deep as the sea.

Photographers Hendrix and Mackey Torres at Fort Macon.

PHOTO CREDITS

The photos on pages 5, 16, 18, 23, 27, 28 are courtesy of the Library of Congress; p. 8 by Corey Balazowich at https://www.flickr.com/coreyann/812700161 and is licensed under the terms of the cc-by-2.0; p. 9 by wozster at https://www.flickr.com/photos/25622789@N00/29568594 and is licensed under the terms of the cc-by-2.0; p. 11 public domain photo at Wikimedia.com by Warfieldian; p. 13 by Kenneth M. Fischer at Wikimedia.com and is licensed under the terms of the cc-sa- by-4.0 intl.; p. 19 by Megan McClinton; p. 26 public domain photo at Wikimedia.com byAaronm86; p. 29 Shutterstock; p. 30 by *Daily Arkansas Gazette*; p. 31 *Carroll A. Deering*. (2023, February 4). In Wikipedia.; p. 34 by Jon Gudorf Photography at Wikimedia.com and is licensed under the terms of the cc-by-2.0; p. 36 public domain photo at Wikimedia.com by U.S. Coast Guard; p. 37 Croatan. (2023, March 6). In Wikipedia.; p. 38 public domain photo at learnnc.org; p. 41 public domain photo at Wikimedia.com by unknown source; p. 43 @roanokeislandinn by Outer Banks Tourism; p.44 at cinematreasures.org; p. 46 by Ken Lund at Wikimedia.com and is licensed under the terms of the cc-by-2.0; p.51 by DrStew82 at Wikimedia.com and is licensed under the terms of the cc-sa- by-4.0; p. 52 public domain photo by Vbofficial at Wikimedia.com; pp. 54 & 55 National Park Service photos @nationalparkservice.gov; p. 56 by Angela Ogilvie Hedgepeth; p. 61 Standard diving dress. (2023, March 16). In Wikipedia.; p. 62 author's personal collection; pp. 63 & 64 by Hendrix and Mackey Torres; p. 67 @thewebblibrary.com; p. 68 by Gerelene Pittillo Metcalf @Facebook.com; pp. 72 & 74 by Carl Griffith at Wikimedia.com and is licensed under the terms of the cc-sa- by-3.0; p. 75 by Henryhartly at Wikimedia.com and is licensed under the terms of the cc-sa- by-3.0; pp. 77, 78, 79, & 81 by Hendrix and Mackey Torres; p. 83 by Beau and Jalayne Torres. ♥

BIBLIOGRAPHY

Bland, Sam. "Of Lifesaving, Life Taking and Ghosts." www.coastalreview.org, June 13, 2016.

Boyd, Sandra. "Virginia Dare and the Lost Colony: Fact and Legend." *Tar Heel Junior Historian,* Spring 2000.

Byers, Thomas. "Ocracoke Haunted Lighthouse Plus Haunted Ocracoke Island With All Its Ghosts." Hub Pages, November 19, 2014.

Cotton, Sallie Southall. *"The White Doe: The Fate of Virginia Dare."* 1901.

Elizabeth, Norma and Bruce Roberts. *Lighthouse Ghosts & Carolina Coastal Legends.* Lighthouse Publications, January 1, 2004.

Fairbank, Dave. "Ghost Stories, legends, and mysteries: The haunted history of the Outer Banks." *The Virginia Pilot,* October 5, 2021.

Fairbanks, Allen. "Is there paranormal activity at the local library?" ABC News Channel 2, November 1, 2019.

Hahn, Amy. "Haunted House on the Hill, Beaufort, North Carolina." www.activerain.com, October 27, 2010.

Hall, Stephanie. "Haunted Spots on the Outer Banks." www.outerbanks.org, September 23, 2022.

Hampton, Jeff. "A bloody feud haunts Kitty Hawk's Black Pelican restaurant." *The Virginian-Pilot,* October 31, 2015.

Haraburda, Lisa. "The Black Pelican." www.blackpelican.com/history.

Harper, John. "End of an era: Manteo's Pioneer Theater closes its doors after more than 100 years." *The Virginia Pilot*, January 9, 2023.

Heit, Judi. "North Carolina Shipwrecks." www.northcarolinashipwrecks.blogspot.com/2012/04.

Howard, Philip. "Augustus Abner McGuire." *Ocracoke Island Journal*, March 17·2011.

_____. *Digging Up Uncle Evans: History, Ghost Tales, & Stories From Ocracoke Island*. Black Squall, 2008.

_____. "Mrs. Godfrey's Ghost." www.villagecraftsmen.com, August 18, 2018.

Lukei, Melina J. "A Brief History of Wash Woods and Beach Area." www.knottsialndheritage.org.

MacDonald, Thomas E. "Ode to Mrs. Godfrey." www.villagecraftsmen.com, Jun 23, 2011.

MacGowan, Doug. "Theodosia Burr Alston Disappearance at Sea." www.historicmysteries.com.

Madia, Tonya and Joey Madia. *Watch Out for the Hallway: Our Two-Year Investigation of the Most Haunted Library in North Carolina*. Visionary Living, Inc., 2018.

McConnel, Rob. "Tanya and Joey Madia—The Haunted Webb Library in Morehead City in North Carolina." The "X" Zone Radio Show, December 20, 2018.

"Old Diver." www.ocracokenavigator.com/old-diver/.

Quine, Katie. "4 Outer Banks Ghost Stories That'll Spook This Halloween." www.ourstate.com, October 7, 2016.

Schmidt, Peggy. *Ghosts of the Outer Banks*. Schiffer Publishing, 2012.

Tabb, Kim. "Mysterious Happenings on the Outer Banks." www.carolinadesigns.com, October 10, 2017.

Twiddy Marketing. "Haunted Outer Banks: Spooky OBX Ghost Stories." www.twiddy.com, October 28, 2021.

Warchol, Alice. "Ghosts of Wash Woods Station." www.visitcurrituck.com, November 2, 2016.

Whedbee, Charles Harry. *Blackbeard's Cup and Stories of the Outer Banks*. Blair Publishing, 1989.

Zacharias, Lee. "A Circle, A Line, An Island: Ocracoke Ghosts." www.ourstate.com/ocracoke-ghosts/, April 29, 2015.

WEBSITES

Morehead City NC: www.moreheadcitync.org

National Park Service: www.nps.gov

NC Ghosts: www.northcarolinaghosts.com

Ocracoke Preservation Society: ocracokepreservationsociety.org

Only in Your State: www.onlyinyourstate.com

Otherworldly Oracle: www.otherworldlyoracle.com

Outer Banks History Center: www.outerbanks.com/history

Roanoke Island Inn: www.roanokeislandinn.com

Twiddy & Company Realtors: www.twiddy.com

Village Craftsmen: www.villagecraftsmen.com

Visit Currituck: www.visitcurrituck.com

Wikipedia: www.wikipedia.com

More from Black Cat Press

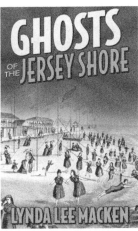

Ghosts of the
Jersey Shore

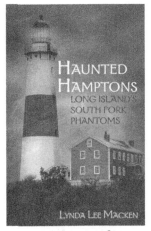

Haunted
Hamptons

Haunted
Cape May

Haunted Long
Beach Island

More from Black Cat Press

Adirondack
Ghosts

Haunted Houses
of New Jersey

Catskill
Ghosts

Haunted Salem
& Beyond

Made in the USA
Middletown, DE
10 April 2023